Inquiries can be sent to:
mayajaepoetry@gmail.com

First, I want to give honor to God for giving me the strength and courage to publish my thoughts, Thank You.

I dedicate this book to my family and friends that always believed I could be more.

Mrs. Ratajski, a true embodiment of what a teacher is supposed to be.

Dr. Stanley, you always saw the bigger picture.

My mom that saw the light from the beginning.

My father who always protected my innocence and kept me young.

Kaiden and Savannah for being my push to do better.

Also to the Brown Girls and Boys that need it.

I hope you enjoy.

My Little Black Book

By: Maya J. Grantham

Part 1: Freshman Year

This is for the She's.
The second mother educators.
The second mother that called
Your biological mother whenever you
Were in big fat trouble.
And your real mother said she would beat yo ass if you
"Forgot to do" or "Forgot at home"
Another God-damn homework!

This is for the “She's”...
Who another elementary school lesson
Couldn't make you any closer,
Where blood and melanin
Are no longer important

The She's that change your life.
The She's that saw your light
in the pitch black of the night.

This is for She.
The LaLas
The second moms
The She's that welcome you
home with open arms.
This is for She.
The women that make Monday your favorite day of the week.
The women, that lifted you when you were too weak.

Mrs."She", Thank you.
Thank you for allowing me to make my
Second home your classroom.
Your laugh music to my ears
And your smile my first tattoo, I'll never forget you.

Or regret all the write ups I signed myself,
The failed tests I hid under my bed,
The books I later told you I barely read,
Or the really long parent teacher conferences.

One of my greatest accomplishments,
The coincidence of being in your class,
Was the start of me discovering my craft,
I am so glad the magic happened,
In your class.

False Ad.

Dear God make me a bird so I can fly far,
Far, far away from here!

Dear God make me a bird so I can fly far,
Far, far away from here!

Dear God make me a bird so I can fly far,
Far, far away from here!

Dear god make me a bird,
so I can fly far,
Far, far away from here.

And if you do it I promise to reimburse you, with my life!
Because it's something about about this world,
That just isn't right!

I pledge allegiance to the flag.
Of the United States of America,
And to the republic, for which it stands
One nation under God,
Indivisible with liberty and justice for some!

See I call that false advertisement,
Because as Americans we advertise liberty and justice for all!
All except the little gay boys, and the
Little gay girls that hide in the corners
Because we all know,
Nobody really wants to be friends
with faggot or the dike!
But why not?!

Don't they walk like we do?
Don't they talk like we do?
But the most important thing is don't they Love just like we do?
So why, as Americans, do we feel we have a say in who can love who?
Why can't he love him and she love her just like I love you!

And we can put the bible in there too.
Man shall not lay with man and
Woman shall not lay with woman and
We can point our judgmental fingers,
And we believe in the scripture
that has nothing to do with us!

But we must think,
Do we believe in the scriptures that say
You are fearfully and wonderfully made,
And you can do all things through Christ that strengthens you?
No!

Because if we did we would have accomplished everything
That the little voices in our heads said we couldn't,
And whether your 100 pounds overweight,
Or 50 pounds underweight
Girls and boys would know they are still beautiful in God's eyes!
Yet we despise the homosexuals
Who are just looking for acceptance!

I think,
This whole situation is false advertisement for teens like me!
Because where are all the political arguments
About fourteen year old girls having body amounts twice their age?!
Where are the political arguments
About boys thinking they can't go anywhere without

Their phone,
Money,
A gun,
Weed,
And some condoms?
This false advertisement is making them
Think everything I do is okay,
Just as long as I'm not gay.

And that makes homosexuals feel like
There's something wrong.
And I think it's a shame that people would
Rather die
Than be who they are.

Dear God,
make me a bird so I can fly far,
far,far away from here.

No Child Left Behind...

They say there's no child left behind
But they left us behind the closed doors
Of our sins,
By ourselves,
Locked the door and said our freedom depends on what we did,
We couldn't bid to live.

I hope Martin doesn't see that we completely ruined his vision!
And the village it took to raise children went through division.
We lost sight of our mission,
And now this generation is being raised by
Each other and music.

Because y'all left us behind.
Gave up hope at the drop of a dime!
Never even looked back to see if we were fine!
But then say there's no child left behind!
No child left behind?
I guess that was for a certain amount of time,
And once you noticed that we make mistakes too,
Our time expired.

I guess that goes for everyone
Except for the girls that as soon as she got pregnant
With her very first child her mom kicked her out!
And the boys that started doing drugs
To fill the void that was left,
When life's cookie cutter cut the shape of his dad out!
No child left behind!
No child left behind?

We were all left behind the cages of our minds,
Because we weren't taught often enough

That our flaws are just fine!
And that this thing called perfection
We won't ever be able to accomplish!
They left us behind so our lights wouldn't shine,
In dark cold alley ways called life!

I'm sure the best the CSI
Couldn't even find all the children,
That have been left behind!
In the constraint of our imagination,
We have been taught to be complacent,
In the distortion of our generation!
No child left behind!
No child left behind?!

We never learned
That the medicine to fix the world could be our voices,
Instead we were always told to stay in our place,
Appearing voiceless.
Nobody ever heard our Humble cries to the skies.
Instead they left us alone in our dark closets
To think about why nothing has been accomplished!

Maybe why the reason All of these children
Are slowly,
Slowly,
Dying.
Because y'all left us behind.

A Letter to My Inner Self,

Dear self,

Thank you for learning to love you,
Unconditionally, with no apologies.
You are the bomb.
Thank you, for learning that not everyone is worth you beauty.
Thank you, for studying your flaws
And teaching yourself to love them
Because they,
Are also apart of making you who you are.

Dear self,

Thank you for building your walls.
Thank you for staying strong.
Allowing your branches to keep stretching out into the light after
Every hurricane that tried to break you.
Thank you,
For growing into more than what
They thought you would.

Dear Self, don't stop.
You're alright.
Don't cry.
Just Smile.

Dear self,

Live your life for what you think
Is right in your mind!
Know, that love is coming.
Know that running out of time is a myth.
Remember that if you were to die tonight you'd be missed,
Because i know sometimes,
You think that you wouldn't.

Dear self,

Remember when you were broken,
Choking on false hopes,
And unfulfilled promises shoved down your throat!
Remember that hurt,
And the promise you made to yourself
You'll never go back to being that person!
Remember you've already learned from it!

Understand that you are enough!
You weren't raised to give up!
Dear self,
On the days you feel like no one loves you,
Remember you finally learned too.

Sincerely, You.

Part 2: Sophomore Year

Contemplating...

You contemplate the loss of past loves like mine isn't good
Enough.
You contemplate the lost relationships
Of fake friends
Like you didn't grow up to be a good man
And create family for yourself.

Contemplation,
Is the haunting of your life,
Mocking what you could have done.
Maybe what you would have done
If things just went a little less to the left.

Maybe everything would be fine
If the girl that now hops
From guy to guy
Would've said yes.
Maybe you could've changed her.
Maybe she was the one
That was made for you,
And I'm the consequence
For your lack of effort
To get her.

You think about the time
Life was a little less hard.
When it wasn't about
Acceptance
Or rejection
Progress or
Regression
Blessings or lessons.

But where would you be,
If you worked for nothing.
Never got your heart broken,
Your pride wasn't tested,
Or if God showed himself
To you so you knew
Who you putting all your faith in?
Contemplate that...

It Rained...

I've learned to cry in silence.
I've learned not to bring attention
To my sorrows because I don't want
People to try and look past the gloss of my eyes
And feel my heart break.

I've learned not to complain
Because at the end of the day,
Who's listening anyway?
I've learned that it's okay to weep,
But don't accept defeat.
I've learned that crying.
Isn't the thing that makes you weak.

It's the exhaustion
From breaking on the inside,
Weeping on the outside.
Hitting rock bottom of your soul,
And not even search
For the strength to rise again.

I've learned that crying
Is like when a snake sheds its skin.
I've learned that crying is the renewing of within.

It rained last night.
And I could feel the drops,
Falling from under my eyelids.
I could relate to the feeling of thunder clashing
Because it feels a lot like a heartbreak.
And I could relate to the pain
Of something being struck by lightning
Because it feels a lot like suicide staring you right,
in your face.

I know what's like.
To be stuck in the dark.
In the dark of your heart,
The dark of your thoughts.

Dancing with the devil to the same damn song.
Because he won't leave you alone!
I'm still in the dark,
Stuck with my thoughts,
But I'll be fine,
I'm searching for my strength to rise.

It rained last night.
And I can still feel it pouring on the inside.

Maybe...We All Learn...

Maybe if you praised the birth of us we would grow up into royalty.
Maybe if you learned to listen,
We would learn,
To speak with authority.
Maybe if you accepted us,
We would learn to love the people we are becoming.

Maybe if your parents
Learned from their parents,
Then you could learn me.
Noticing, that time changes with waves crashing.
Maybe if you learned I'd be able to teach,
Lead correctly.
It's kind of hard to hear the strength of my voice,
When it's been belittled to whispers by Mr.Wormwoods.
I'm smarter than what they teach me,
I'm bigger than what you call me because I grow everyday,
And more times then none am I right if you'd only listen.

Maybe,
I'd be able to hear you if you'd only talk to me.
Did you ever notice,
That loud sounds put people on defense mode?
Fire Alarms tell you to leave.
Sirens only tell you to move out of the way,
Alerts on TVs signify storms coming.
The most important messages you get in life,
That will change your mind
Are the ones you get in the dark when you can't sleep.

Or the oceans whispering to you inspiringly.

Maybe, you should learn to be sorry.
Maybe you should reminisce,
Back to the days you used to cry and say when you had kids,
You would never treat them how your parents did.
Now when you discipline me, all you can say is
“Don’t I sound just like my mother did?”,
And you hated it.

I'm scared to become a parent.
And I know I'm probably too young to even think of it,
But I'm scared because it seems like becoming a guardian,
Automatically makes you a hypocrite.

Like y'all never did things and later on regretted it.
You never experimented.
Dibbled and dabbled into toxic chemicals that got
Smoked,
Toked,
Passed off,
You choke,
On the lies you tell.

Never worked so hard and studied so long
To make your dreams come true.
Until you realized that fast money is not,
Dream chasing.
Don't want me to be like you.

Want me to chase my dreams,
Don't worry about love
Because it only leads to heartbreak.
Want me to save your pieces
Of wisdom as keepsakes
For me to keep safe.

Maybe we all learn.
To trust the experiences
We go through on our own,
So we can grow,
As individuals.

But also, put our pride to the side,
Admit when our parents were right,
And one day,
We’re all going to come off a little hypocritical.
To those, we love the most.
Our own…

Playing Games...

Hide and seek let's play
Let's hide from the people
That were supposed to protect us.
The people that are supposed to be with us,
And never against us!

Cops and robbers let's play.
Let's play cops and robbers,
And have have no thieves
Cause no matter the title,
You would still have the power,
To take the life, of the innocent.

Ring around the rosy let's play,
Let's run around in circles,
Singing that once loved tune,
That they sang when that
Deadly disease was being spread by blood sucking bites,
But young black men can never be immune,
To intense stinging bullet wounds!

The Game of Life let's play.
But let's replace all the job opportunities with
Rappers,
Scammers,
And hustlers.
And every card that said..
"Congrats you got a kid in the oven!"
Will now say I'm sorry,
Your baby just got jumped,
And one of those punks pulled out a gun and shot your son!
Move back two spaces!

How about we play monopoly,
And every piece of property be a
Marijuana leaf,
A cup of lean,
And a bad rappers mixtape from down the street,
And every chance card be some news coverage.
About another shootout that took the life of another one of our teens.
Life's a game,
And forget winning,
it’s hard enough just trying to finish.

Sadly there's no cheat codes,
No hints,
No reset button,
Not even pause to get together your thoughts,
Prepare your heart for the next level.
Can't get on base and protect yourself from the Devil.
You just gotta make change to your world,
Have faith,
And know that you will come out successful.
So Let's play.

Interlude: They May Be Lying to You.

When I was in middle school, they told me that I needed the things they were teaching me for high school. They said that it was only going to get more and more difficult and I needed to be ready. In middle school they allowed us to learn but still be creative and express ourselves, so that we could make connections and remember what we learned. In middle school they paid attention to our mood changes and our lacking. The one thing that they told me in middle school that was accurate about my high school experience and on, is that every year the teachers are going to get more and more carefree. Not every teacher is a good teacher and is in it for the love of kids, and their learning. They aren't gonna care if you're on time or late, or even if you come.

As a senior in highschool I've learned that being in advanced classes isn't really about the fact you are advanced or not, it's just so you feel like you're apart of "a club". In middle school they said every year will get harder, but i've read the same books at least twice throughout high school, just to take a quiz on it and say I did it. If you were to ask me now what the books were about, I probably would be able to tell you the bare minimum of what happened, but if you were to ask me about books I've read on my own, I could give you every detail. The most important things you do, are the things you do for yourself. Not the things you do for a grade, or so your teacher can have bragging rights when they're being observed or it's time for state testing. Nothing I've done in school will say that I'm advanced, but the creative things I did in middle school to learn the material before the quiz, will tell you how I got to where I am.

As senior in highschool I learned that education is important, but school in my opinion is not, because a lot of things I learned that have affected my life, didn't happen in a classroom. I think it's because now teachers are more concerned about teaching us about the legends, then making us feel we could be one. Reading the classics, but not finding books that could change the way we look at life. As middle school graduates I encourage you to do everything you can to excel in school, I encourage you to read the classics and listen to the documentaries filled with things we really don't know about the legends. I encourage you to take the quizzes and read the chapters even though after it doesn't matter. I encourage you to do your best, but don't let them brainwash you.

Some keys to success in high school are:

1. Be Yourself
2. Understanding that "Peer Pressure" only works if your weak minded.
3. Bullying only works if you bully yourself.
4. You're not going to need most of the things they teach you.
5. Listen to your heart.
6. If you work for it, you'll get it.
7. Keep your circle small, but mind open.
8. Be involved.
9. Manage your time.
10. Make it an experience.

Thank you for your time, I enjoyed talking to you and I hope you create your own education, and read your classics, and become a Legend.

Part 3: Junior Year

Education Is The Key...

I hate being in AP LIT.
I hate being labeled advanced when really
There's no way anyone could know.
I hate wasting my time.
And I hate reading about the legends,
That nobody really knows existed,
And delaying my grind to become one.

I hate disappointing my family.
I hate seeing the look in my mother's eyes
At the time that probably thinks
I'm the biggest disgrace in her life.
And father shaking his head
Because he's been tapped out for a while.
I'm sorry I can't push through the classics
Aor an "A" on my report card or to see you smile.

I promise I've tried it,
I promise there's been nights
When I wasn't on my phone
I was reading in silence,
But there was just too much time
Between the action in the book that kept me excited
And the dream under my eyelids.

I hate being in AP Lit.
I hate reading things that didn't change my life.
Or made me feel important,
Like my junior year when Mr. Williams made me read
Tuesday's With Morrie.
Because Morrie taught me to accept what
I CAN do and what I CAN'T because both
Equally make me who I am.
He taught me to forgive others,
And don't feel that it's too late to get involved with my craft.
Morrie taught me to always make sure I'm at peace with myself.

To create my own culture,
That death is one thing to be sad over,
But to look back on your life and realize
You lived and stood for nothing is something else.

Without Mrs.Ratajski's
I would've never written a poem.
I would've never found a way to express my
Cries or even my smiles.
I would've never got into reading anything other
Than what I was told to and sometimes not even those.
I would've never been open to learn without her classroom
Because her's was the only one that didn't
Make me feel like I was walking into a jail cell.

I hated being in AP lit because it was just
Something to do for bragging rights.
To be apart of a "club" that nobody knew about.
I hated being in AP Lit because that class,
Never made me think,

I never felt unique,
Because when I looked at the
Freshman's side of the board,
Don't you know they were learning
The exact same thing?

Stories...

She always told me stories about when she was as a teen.
How she was walking the street,
To her own little beat
Not realizing
That the sound was coming from her mother's
Heels she had on her feet
Touching the concrete.

Stories about how she would get
Aroused dirty stares from men older than her,
Cause she had on her tight little dress
Like the ones we wear now
Because styles always seem to come back around.

And she would always explain what they
Thought about her figured silhouette under sheets.
And that a dead man on a piece of paper
Was how they came to meet,
Green was her favorite color.

But she never told stories
About how she would have true love feelings,
And how her man didn't want anything more
Than to know what she's thinking.
But just about dirty old men wanting,
Sexual healing.
Just stories about how she would walk up and down
Mt.Ephraim, because her home was lethal,

There wasn't a place she could step
Without stepping on a needle.
Maybe that's why
She always kept her heels on.

Maybe she thought that those
5 extra inches kept her above all her issues,
And she she was never taught to be a woman
And deal with them.

But mommy I'm down here!
And You put me in a pair of 5 inch heels.
Kinda like the ones you and grandma used to wear.
Now I get my own little stares,
But not from grown men,
Just little boys that wanna be.

But I'm not like you!
I've just learned from what I've seen.
So how dare you have the audacity to criticize me?!
Tell me I shouldn't show what shouldn't seen.
When your legs have extended across this country,
And your sorrows are deeper
Than the Caribbean Sea?!

Mom you hate me because
When you look at me, the only thing you see is green.
And the fact that you see all of yourself in me.
So tell me your stories,
Take your heels off,
And if you want to you drown me in your sorrows.

Have You?

Have you ever been scared of the person
That reminds you you're beautiful
Just in case you forgot?

The person that cares
Enough to call you throughout their day?
Have you ever been so scared
Of the person that takes
Concern out of walking distance?
Because anything else would be too fast,
Getting you to the point of separation,
But you can't stand watching another
Person leave you?

Have you ever,
Been so scared of the person that makes
Hours worth of talking not seem like enough?

And you want to call their bluff,
For a quick second the idea passes
Your mind that they just might be perfect...
But then you go back to being scared
Because you then realize that,
Nobody is.

Have you ever,
Tried to put makeup on all your flaws so all of you seems
So level and even toned & Just so damn beautiful.

But one day you know,
Just maybe,
You two, will spend the night together.
And all that makeup has to come off.
Have you ever been so scared,
But so in love
With the real you,
That you can't even fathom someone else
Seeing it and loving you too?
I have.

Keep Me Grounded...

Ain't it sad I still don't know my truth?
I can't even pick specific family leaves
Off of my family tree to even know where my
Roots begin.
Fallen leaves turned to dust,
Dirt that they walk upon,
My family tree they...hung us on.
I'll never know if it's in my blood line to be a icon,
And I'll never know if the people I did learn about
Were led to light on behalf of my ancestors.
On behalf of... pieces of me.
I am not my sister's keeper, I am my sister.
We all have the same strength but,
Not the same courage lift your voice,
Or get pushed to the dirt,
By those who are scared for us to know who we are.

Forever we stand,
In the dark.
So they can't see the faces of those who
Are strong enough to fight against them,
Locked and bound together cause that's all we have
And sometimes,
We barely even have that.
Forever we stand, unheard and mistaught.
The simple thought of us
Knowing who we are is enough to change the heart
Of America.

Because we know,
That they know,
That we know if we actually knew
The truth about ourselves,
There'd be no further stopping us.
No more blind leading the blind.
And those lighter than us,
Trying to tell us, and teach us,
How...to be black.

Listen..

A mouth that chooses not to speak
Is one that accepts defeat ,
Has eyes that can not see
Where they're really meant to be,
And ears that can only hear the fear
In their own mind.

Being deaf and blind probably makes to speechless,
Because you can't even follow
The signs that speak to you.
Wake Up!
Dreams and Nightmares
Are only distractions from the fact
That you are still stuck in the dark alone.

Are you hearing me?
Are you listening?
You are not broken nor breaking your changing.
Learning,
That being bitter is not apart of the process
Of accepting you are alone,
You are not lonely.

It's just quite because you're moving in silence.
He's probably thinking that you're still
Chasing behind him,
But you're faster than that.
Yeah you might of fell once or twice,
Had a couple tears fall from your eyes

While your conscience told you
These boys don't love you stop trying.
And he don't care so stop crying...
Keep grinding,
Keep smiling,
Keep loving,
Keep shining
Don't break no sweat,
Just catch your breath & keep going.

And when it feels like you're the diamond in the rough.
When it feels like what you give
Is never enough,
Know that stars are conceived in your eyes,
The moon borrows beauty from the shine in your smile.
To someone You...
Are everything!

Self Doubt...

I've been gone for a while.
I've been sitting back trying
To figure out how to improve my style.
Sitting back thinking is writing poetry really worth while?
Wondering if the things I spit really
Triggered a thought or a smile.
Wondering if parents felt like if their teens
Watched me it would change their life!

Wondered if I should just stop and make room
For the more serious writers.
Those that spit lyrical venom to the audience!
The poets.
Those that Rhyme on the bus cause
Something triggers their mind!
Those that lose half their stuff in the air
Because they never wrote it down!
Those that had Dr.Seuss like rhyming Slam battles,
With their friends that thought they were a better
Spoken word artist.

I've been Gone for a while.
Running and hiding
Ducking and dodging those that just
Wanted to hear one more rhyme.
The people that always
Seemed to remember the time I came at Nicki Minaj!
I've been gone, but I'm back now.
I've realized that writing is my only way to break out.

And it didn't change but it saved my life!
I'm back now, Maya the Poet,
Insight, and occasionally Da Monster!
I'm sorry for the wait.
But you can call me *Maya JAE, The Poet.*

Space

Between

Us...

I see your face in the sky all the time.
And even though it's supposed to more of a thunderstorm,
You're more like a shooting star.
I wished on you.
Wished that you were the star that would glow for me,
Be my light in the dark times,
But you passed me by without a trace,
No line.
You made me realize,
I'm too old for stars.
I deserve the moon.

12 long hours of the day that's not visible
To the human eyes,
But it's always been
There to greet me,
The night,
When I need it the most.
Unlike you,
A shooting star,
Pop up at the worst times

Then leave before I could've had a closer look .
But still you would insist on me
Making space for you in my life.
Darling..
Stars explode and create black holes .

Damn no wonder my heart’s an abyss.
Maybe that's why your kisses were so
Empty and your eyes were always blank,
You were never whole like the moon,
Or really here to be the light to my dark sky
That wasn't really all that dark in first place.
You just wanted to be wished on.

Baby, thank you for the lesson that
When you wish for shooting stars,
Sometimes all you get is airplanes.
Maybe I knew that.
Maybe,
I just wanted to pretend,
Pretend you could be more to me than what you were to them.
I'll rely on the moon's dim light then
To ever trust a shooting star again
Because shooting stars fade,
Without a line or trace.
And sometimes...
Get mistaken for airplanes.

Sweet Dream

One time.
I dreamt of a lady with a heart of gold.
It shined so bright, and was pure as snow.
Her skin was smooth and so beautiful, it glowed.
More intense than the moon in an empty sky.
Her eyes, shined bright like the stars,
So I no longer wondered where I had gotten mine.
She told me,
Her name was Mom.

The very first thing that came to mind,
Was how could God allow an angel
So divine drop down from the sky?
In the body of a Queen, head held high.
Energy so strong it could crack the ground we walk upon.
Spirit brighter than a summer's day.
I dreamt of a Women.
A women that shined brighter than the moon she loved,
And the stars she had fallen from.
I dreamt of an Angel, she told me her name was Mom.

She told me she would be there to wipe the tears from my eyes.
She said she was there to make me wise.
This is a woman, that for her I would die.
I would climb Mount Everest a thousand times
If that meant that she could live her life without the stress of time.
I dreamt of a Woman with the strongest of minds.
I am her flower child.

Part 4: Times Up...

HEY KING...

This is for the boys that think even trying to be a decent human
Being is gay.
That think expressing your feelings is soft.
And a rough tough thug NIGGA
Is what us good girls want.
This is for the boys..
That smoke so much weed to keep
Their eyes so low so they never see the light.
The light of the sun the light of life!
Does weed keep your cries silent?
Does the lean you drink keep you safe from falling too short?
I'm talking to the boys.

You tell me, it's not like a lady to provide for herself.
You say it's a man's job.
You tell me, it's not like a lady to stand up for herself.
You say it's a man's job.
But ain't I a lady?
Didn't it take God to create me to complete you?
Ain't I a lady?
Who silhouette is enough to get any man
To bring down the moon, just so It can admire me?
Ain't I a lady?
Don't my power move mountains?!
Don't my voice pump the blood in ya heart?!
Ain't I a lady?

And Ain't you scared?!
Don't you want me weak?!
Ain't you a boy?
You watch me from a distance not wanting to say
The wrong thing to a lady like me.
But ain't you The Man?
Ain't you the one who brag to your friends
How you can get any walking thing?
But don't I stand by myself?
Seeing through your game, because my last guy
Gave me the cheat codes to your kind.
Ain't you here to play me?

But ain't I too good?!
My skin too smooth, you hug me and forget why
you approached me in the first place.
I look at you, straight faced, ain't you gonna lie?
I'll wait,
Because I know it's coming.

"Yo, I think I seen you before",
But how when I work more the a field negro.
No boy you ain't seen me nowhere.

Don't you wish you had?
Before your father taught you to walk over
Women like the London bridge.
So you would know how to appreciate me,
Like you wish he did your mother.

I'm talking to the boys.
That boys that want to be men!
But can't say they're sorry,
And understand that when
It comes to us women they don't need their defense!
We are the ones who kisses mend broken hearts.
The ones who don't judge when tears drop like falling
Stars.

The women, you try to come back to
After Karma has broken your heart.

It's time to make change.
Realize you have a choice.
You don't have to let circumstances make you,
They will be the same ones to break you.
You have a voice.

No real woman will let you
Lead them because you were lead
By broken men.
Who thought if they played tough,
They would never get mistaken for their father
Who they thought was a weak man.

But playing tough looks
Worse than tapping out
Because at least he could
Admit to his shortcomings,
While you're still trying to pretend.
This, is for the boys,
I hope it helps you find yourself.

10:02 PM Thoughts...

I wonder if my tears were acid would I still cry.
I wonder if they burned my face coming down,
Would you still pull the trigger for them to fall from my eyes.
I wonder.

I wonder if the broken pieces of my heart
Found their way outside of me,
Would you take them too?
Would you take every piece and try to recreate the heart I used to.
The one that skipped beats at sight of you.
The one that accepted lies from you.
The one that you broke in the first place, but I had to fix.

But if you break a mirror and fix it,
Don't you still see the cracks in it?
I wonder.

Shouldn't you see yourself shattered
In the reflection of my broken heart,
You say love me right?
I wonder if that's true...

I wonder if I stopped wondering then would you care?
Would you wonder why I stopped texting,
And where have I been?
Wonder if I'm alright and if I made it back back in?

If it were me who finally stopped giving a fuck,
Would you then realize it was you
That missed out on your luck.

Your luck with a girl
who was down and wasn't trying to misuse.
A girl that wasn't playing and would give her life for you.
A girl that would always be there till death do us part.
A girl that always said I love you, before hanging up,
And you never had to guess if it came from the heart.

See I read a tweet once, you know that relationship shit,
It said "There's a big difference between giving up
and knowing when you've had enough".
I wonder what this is.

I wonder if I'm finally tired of being last on your mind.
I wonder If I'm tired of begging for you to change this time.
I wonder if I ran out of acid to cry.
I wonder if my pain showed on the outside,
Like a scar or a bruise,
Would you still chose to do the things that you do.

It's 10:02, and I'm sorry,
But I don't think I have any tears left for you.

Black and White

I have,
Questions in my eyes.
I have the answers in my mind,
And your invitation is in the curve of my spine.
Are you coming?
I'll wait here.

You can't see me,
You're blind to the gold that lets my skin shimmer,
I glow.
You're ashamed of your own,
But I know.
You praise me in private, at the crack of pure nighttime,
You wish, the figures of your imagination
Held you like I did.
The one, that came closest to comforting
Your sorrows as best as your mother,
But do you hate her too?
Do you hate the brown in her skin?
The power of the syllables that leave her lips,
Do hate the motion in her hips?
Do you hate the woman that created you?
Do you look at her and regret her like you do me?
Does she you?

I, am the only one that purely loved the glisten in your eyes,
The strength of your soul,
I'd worship the ground you'd walk on.
But only after I did my own.
I was prepared for you to leave me,
So I made sure I had something to stand on with all ten toes.

I lost myself in my wrinkled sheets,
In the Hollow of my being.
In the darkness of my thoughts,
That only seemed to be about you,
And our nighttime encounters,
That lead to the climax of our visit, you, leaving me.
In the dampness of your selfishness, me being naive,
I longed for your touch that burned from the inside,
But was so bitter sweet.

I found myself,
Finding myself.
And knowing I was enough.
My Solitude meant more to me then your
False Company.
I never left myself.

In every puddle,
Of blood,
Sweat or tears,
Sometimes all three.
I was the one who picked myself up.
Because,
"The strength of a woman is not measured by the
Impact that all her hardships in life have had on her;
But the strength of a woman is measured by the extent of her
Refusal to allow those hardships to dictate her and
Who she Becomes."

I will not,
Let you tell me who and what I should be.
Because I,
Am a woman.
I, am set up the same way as the one,
Who created,
Carried and made you what you are.
The man, that has too much pride to swallow,
He chokes.
The man who hangs himself with his very own rope of
Hypocrisy,
Arrogance, and belittlement of one's self.

It is you who does not feel they are enough to please me,
The woman who raises you by herself.
We, never needed the help of your kind to make change,
Survive and provide.
You just lost sight of yourself and forgot
It was essentially your job.
We were created to provide you with what
Was missing from your dreams.
Pieces of you are inside of we.

We are created to complete you,
You are now incomplete.
And your missing piece is inside of me.

Or maybe I just wanted it to be...

DIARY OF AN ABG...

Hello, my name is Maya and I live in the generation
Where having my thick hair should be a sin.
A generation where I can't walk into a room
Without automatically being perceived as rude
Because I don't smile.
I don't like speaking to everybody.
Guys don't like me because I'm too strong.
I don't fall for anything.
Not even sweet nothings because I know the difference.
Where do you think this face came from?
I've learned the truth the hard way.
That not everybody is in it with me the long way,
You're looking the wrong way
If you looking at me to break myself down,
Contemplating on how I can be enough for you!

I accept being the ANGRY BLACK GIRL..
Because I refuse to hold my tongue for you!
I refuse to allow Lupita to be the only
Example of my black is beautiful!
I have every right to be angry!
To act Painless, your words don't cut me!
My skin ain't that thin!
You try to break me don't ya?
Tell me my hair too nappy.
My wit is too quick,
Tongue to sharp, spit like acid!
I burn you with my honesty you weren't ready for me!

I accept your challenge of being angry.
Because you made me!
LIGHT ENOUGH to be considered cute,
But attitude still black enough to remind you where you come from!
You question me too,
Like why black girls gotta be so mean?
Why black girls always so loud?
Why black girls so insecure?
Why black girls always gotta be so strong,
Like y'all can't just relax learn to stay in
Y'all lane and play y'all part?

When truthfully, black girls aren't mean we're raw,
We're tired of trying to be nice because look where that got us!
We loud because we're finally tired of being quieted down!
The sound of our voice burns coming out
Because y'all missed some of the fire in it
When you tried to put it out,
Tried to shut us down!

We're insecure because our bottled up Black Girl magic,
Gets stolen everyday,
And black boy would rather the store brand over the actual thing.
That's like buying Bunch O" Cinnamon Squares
Over Cinnamon Toast Crunch.
Black Girls so strong because we have to be!
Knowing if we let y'all break us,
It'll be like going all the way back to slavery working
For the mercy of a man,
But let us not forget,
White men WHIPPED y'all too!

Society and their beauty standards
Didn't just brainwash some of us,
But brainwashed you!

Pay attention,
Kim K's boxer braids
Are the same thing black girls had in like third grade,
But why is she exotic and "setting trends"
But we gotta be Harriet Tubman!
We're strong because we have to protect what we
Bring to the table remembering that's what we built the table for!

I accept your challenge of being the **ANGRY BLACK GIRL,**
Angry black woman, angry black Queen.
Because it is not about me being angry,
It's me taking a bite of my apple,
Getting smacked by the harsh winds of the world and realizing,
That's the only way to be.
So you can take me seriously not wanting to
Raise a black son to step on my back just to disrespect
A newer generations me.

So again,
I accept your challenge in being **ANGRY.**

Polaroid...

Picture this,
you move in slow motion.
Every look and every notion.
Every sight and every detail,
Takes you 10,000 times longer to notice it
Then a normal person.
Your brain doesn't get the message
Fast enough to tell the muscles in your arms,
Hands and finger
Between your pointer and your ring to wake up,
Move with a purpose,
You have to tell the world something,
Fuck You.

No scratch that.
You are perfectly fine.
But the world is stuck in fast forward.
So everyone is moving too fast
Trying to keep up with time
To have time to stop and notice
That actually you're crying.
Actually you're screaming
. Actually you're dying.
You're shattered.
And as everyone races by
They're actually stepping on broken pieces
Of your mind & of your pride.
You are a being in this world that is blind to your light.

Nope actually scratch that!
You perfectly fine
And so is the world around you.
Just nobody cares.
Nobody cares about themselves
Let alone care about the lie they told you
To act on it and to keep it going.
The lie being they care about you.
But everything is fine.
Your mind is just crowded with too many lies.
Lies of tender love and care that's supposed to
Be in store for you.
But every store you go to they seem to be out of stock.
So you have to learn to love yourself and with this education
You find that that's the most important kind.

This world was not created to love you,
In fact it was created to trick you into believing
That the wrong people do.
It's your job to scratch that,
Build your own world full of atoms
And learn to appreciate what was given to you and work
With what you have.
Play the cards you were dealt,
keep your own thoughts in your back pocket and not
The ones they think you should have.
Never change or exchange them
Because they might short change you,
And your mind to think something
was missing from your life.
When all you needed, is what you got.

Fairy Tales...

They tell us as princesses that if a boy is mean to us,
He likes us.
They tell us that they mature a little slower,
They can't express themselves and they're just a little too rough.
They tell us that these things are okay
As long as it's not too much.
But is not too much
A clutch to the neck or a punch in the gut?

I know a girl.
Who has a father she probably thinks doesn't love her.
But a man that tells her he does.

I know a girl who is okay with being abused
As long as she has no responsibilities.
Buckling knees.
Broken glasses.
Wrestling around generating noise greater
Than stampedes and it's just the two of them,
He bruises her.
Or she bruises herself.
Taken responsibility blames it on age difference.
He bruises her.
Uses her, I know a girl.

That doesn't love herself enough,
Pretends to feel beautiful even when she's by herself.
I know a girl.
That allows a man to downplay her.
Degrades herself.
He Stripped her of her wings just to dance with him,
The Devil.
Turned her into villain.
Maleficent,
He only steals from her because he sees her potential.

I know a girl.
That looks into the mirror and lies to herself!

You're gonna okay!
It's gonna be better
He loves you!
He didn't mean it
No one will notice.
It's not that bad

I know a girl.
I know a Queen.
That can't even run her own kingdom because she's too content
With being a peasant in a mans world.
Baby girl, you are too beautiful
To be walked upon,
To be treaded on.
Stand up on your own!
I know a girl.
Who is afraid to love herself.
Alone.

A Message For Justin...

I hope this message gets to you in time.
Before your wings reach their fullest development, your alarm clock goes off indicating Freedom Time and your spirit starts to fly, I appreciate the calmness within you. Listening to your voice is like watching the sun rise in the morning while the ocean tides are still calm. It's like finally finding the peace within your own spirit, within your own mind.
It's like being able to look in the mirror say that you're beautiful and meaning it this time.

I'd never, thought I'd had to say goodbye to you. And I'd never thought you'd speak my name and I'd find out "in memory" of you, never thought I'd Minister for and not to you! But I hope this message gets to you in time, that I love your smile and the life in your eyes. I love the world you'd escape to when you start to sing, and I love the music notes you use for wings. I know that Gods missed you in his choir, and he probably uses you to sing him lullabies.

I hope this message gets to you in time, that I heard about your wife, I heard she gives you more than butterflies. She gives you the life God meant for you. You two, are a match made in your new home, I heard, that her silhouette under your bed sheets, she being perfectly imperfect is what you loved about her. I heard that her crown of curls was always left wild, not able to be pinned down, giving her that perfect pitch of rich sounds.

I heard, that she's helped you live, she's helped you give to us more than what she's given to you, I heard you're in love with a women, named music. Her race is acoustic, she a beautiful match for you. I feel bad for the Island Girl that didn't get to snatch you before she did, but I'm happy she didn't because I'm not too sure if the Island Girl would've been able to give me chills such as Music does. I heard to you say she's The One.

I hope this message gets to you in time, that I'm better cause I've known you, to heaven you will soar to, and I pray that you know, you're always gonna hold this permanent place in my heart.

My Type...

I like Brown Boys..
Dark chocolate,
Milk chocolate,
Toffee,
Almond & or caramel
Are my favorite flavors of candy and romantic partners.
Y'all are the best thing Willy Wonka **EVER** created in his chocolate factory.
Y'all are my Golden Ticket...
To heartbreak.

I hate,
That y'all are so smooth,
Sweet when you chose to be,
Succulent and divine,
Delicious and nutritious,
Filled with Vitamin D-estruction of my self esteem.

I never seemed worthy of your faithfulness.
You were never proud to have me to lean on!
Even though,
I held you when you cried
And didn't even tell you to man up,
Because it's my type of guy to not have
Too much pride & admit when he needs help!

Take some of the confidence
He's invested in himself and put ome into us!
But I was never worth it.

I remember when,
One of my closest friends asked me
"Maya, why is it that the guys you like never seem to like you?"
As I stood there hurt,
Not by what she said,
Just by the fact there was someone else
Besides myself that drew this same conclusion.
I thought,

Maybe because I have a type.

I always fall for the same flips and tricks,
Lies and excuses that came from my type.
My Brown Boys that have no genuine like for my type.
They only like us when we're "winning" or "in season"

Maybe
Because I should start practicing
What I preach and stop believing in time.
Realize,
I might not be married be 25,
And I won't have my kids by the end of my prime.
Because my type of guys,
Aren't likely to stick around.

Because my type of guys,
Are only good to do three things
Cheat,
Steal and Lie.

Cheat...
Me out of smiles and cries and sometimes
Those happen at the same damn time.
Cheat me out of long nights.
Nights that I'm up thinking of where the relationship is going,
While you're asleep, dreaming of ways to end it.

But little do you know your mother,
Is always gonna ask you where have I been,
And when is she gonna see me again?
Your father,
Will invite me over for dinner even when we come to an end,
Because real eyes realize real lies.
They are going to see that I'm real
While the whole time you're blind!

My type,
Steal daydreams and nightmares
Because in them both, they, are my savior!
They steal places in my heart and always
Leave something behind for me to remember them by,
Even though I just want to forget.

They cheat on the promises
Just to give mine to someone else,
And in this generation,
I wouldn't be surprised if it were one of my "friends".
Cheat on my custom love poems written just for them.

My type of guys,
Cheat on my mind with one less complex,
One they don't have to work as hard for.
Cheat on my heart that they never yearned for
In the middle of the night,
Scratch that, the middle of the day.
Yearned my heart enough to schedule a romantic date even
though it's only for his hour lunch break.

My type of guys,
Can go all day without me even
Crossing his mind just one time.
My type.
My Brown Boys.
Don't value the stars I conceive in my palms,
Don't acknowledge the sun rays in
My soul or the gems in my mind.

So the next guy I meet,
That can act out this piece,
Without ever having to read it.
I'll have to tell them,
I'm sorry, you're just not my type...

It's Time!

Everybody has a life purpose.
But nobody seems to want to find their own.
They're too busy trying to make
Fast money with dime bags and stripper poles.
Or writing wack ass bars trying to be the clone of a rapper,
Who is the clone,
Of a clone, of a clone
Of a rapper.

Digging themselves deeper and deeper
Into life holes of wasted time and depression.
Then they look up and realize that their greatest highs
Are still low because they still aren't whole.
They still don't know what they're actually hear for,
Who they are and if they could be more!

Their heart,
burns with the urge to free themselves
Out of life's jail cell.
Did you eat, their false dreams too fast?
Did you let them feed your mind
With the lie that they are not using us,
For target practice,
That black lives do matter?
Did you let them finesse you of your voice,
were you the Ariel to the Ursalas?
Did you allow yourself to be shriveled up,
Like raisins in the baking sun,
So they can stand up?

They,
are never going to fight for us!
You,
Are the only soldier in your army
But don't rely on no gun,
Life and death are in the power of your tongue.
Speak up,
Ask for what you want!
Speak life into what you need!
They're feeding us Misbeliefs,
Stay Mad,
Stay Woke!
Stay pissed off,
At your at your culture for staying enslaved!
Staying in Jordans,
I mean Nike,
I mean Rollies,
I mean Louis V,
I mean Gucci,
I mean chains,
Staying in chains!

Getting whip flashed to the end,
the back of the bus, they keep our truth hushed!
Stay loud!, about how you feel!

Don't ever!,
Let anyone tell you that the sky's the limit,
Because if that was the case astronauts
Would've met **God** already!
The goal is the heavens!
I'm gone grind to get mine,
To meet God,
since **NASA's** limit is the sky
I'm gonna make that only one of mine!
Not that I can be limited,
I'm never finished and neither should you.
Just keep pushing through,
Find your peace of mind, and learn to love you.
Because that is your purpose.

You Shine TOO Brown Girl...

We shouldn't be the black holes
That get to share the same space
With the stars who actually made it.
Because they wouldn't even ***shine as bright***
If we all were as light as them!

Brown girl,
Don't collapse onto yourself
Wishing that you weren't blessed
With the treasure that other girls are
Searching for,
You are a gold mine!

Your mind,
Holds the magic tricks on how to dance on water,
Lay on the moon!
You,
Are in an exclusive relationship with the sun.
He kisses you everyday,
That's what keeps you so golden!

They lay there begging for love his rejection burns them,
They weren't created to be like you!
Move with you,
The sway in your hips is the like
When the tide is high
They can't even swim with you!

Don't you see we're switching places?
We bleach while they tan,
They enhance their features
While well,
We'll shake what our mamas gave us
Cause that's the only thing that keeps
Us in the race for the attention of a man,
But they're laughing at you...

Brown Girl...
you don't only shine as bright,
but you are the night sky that holds them them up!
You are the blueprint to where they get their light from!
Enlighten them,
Enlighten yourself,
On the queens that made you who you are.

No one, can love you if you hate yourself.
Stop blaming yourself for them
Not being able to see the
Diamonds in your eyes,
The strength in your hair,
And the power in your stride
Because Brown boy doesn't even have
A play in his book
On how to love himself.
They copy cat off copy cats then tell you they're different.
Brown boy doesn't understand how to live.
Taught to walk in fear.
Fear to cry,
Fear to think,
But no fear to die.

They want a girl to do it.
Brown boy,
Wants any girl to be his ride or die besides,
The one that look like their momma.
Because brown girl, ain't good enough.

Brown girls are are here to live up,
Higher than the stars.
We will not be torn apart,
Brown girls are strong because our mothers taught us,
Prepared us for the truth.
That you shouldn't depend on the world
To be the only thing to love you.

The Secrets Out...

Dear "Friends",
I'm sorry that maybe I wasn't stable enough.
I'm sorry that my problems mixed with your problems,
And theirs was just a little too much.
Not that i couldn't be there or wasn't, or didn't care
As much...
I'm just saying i gave you what I had, all of it.
I never shortchanged, or rearranged so that I carried
ones weight more than the other, I gave all of you all
of me.
But maybe I couldn't worry about relationships that
weren't mine,
Because to this very day I'm still trying to figure out
Why all the guys I like never like me.
Still trying to figure out, why no ones sees that i'm
trying.
Still trying to figure out why God made me so strong
But I'm always fucking crying, I'm still crying!
And i'm still trying to figure out why the hell i'm here if
no one
Sees me anyway...
Always wondering, if i do,
take this razor blade to my skin,
How am i gonna explain it when I need it edited away.
Still trying to figure out why time is going by so fast,
Relationships don't last,
My head burns and my heart, hurts.

Most importantly, I'm still trying to figure out,

How I have all of these friends,
But no one sees that their broken friend is still breaking,
Picking up the broken pieces to put herself
Together again because no one will help her do it,
She's still pressing.

Dear "Friends",
I don't want you to help me,
I don't want any handouts.
Sometimes, I just need you to listen.
Sincerely, so i'm not just talking to myself.
Even though I'll probably still talk to myself
Because then i'll know for sure
that someone is actually listening.
Don't pity me.
Don't fix me.
Just know, I never want you to feel how I feel.
Think what I think.
I never, want you to love being by yourself
Because then no one can leave you.
But being scared of yourself because you're so close,
To leaving you too.

Dear "friends",
The Secrets Out.
And I hope that me helping me,
Will help you.

"POET BREATHE NOW,
BECAUSE IT IS THE
LAST THING YOU WILL
EVER DO FOR
YOURSELF..."
– ADAM GOTTLIEB

www.ingramcontent.com/pod-product-compliance
Ingram Content Group UK Ltd.
Pitfield, Milton Keynes, MK11 3LW, UK
UKHW041921190726
13854UKWH00003B/1366

9 781387 669646